Horn Book's

LAURA INGALLS WILDER

*Articles about and by Laura Ingalls Wilder,
Garth Williams and The Little House Books*

Little House on the Prairie
Independence, Kansas

Edited by William Anderson

ACKNOWLEDGEMENTS

The editor wishes to note the assistance of Anita Silvey, editor of *The Horn Book Magazine* of Boston for arranging permission to bring back into print these classic articles of Wilder lore.

Special thanks are in order to Garth Williams, for his elaborations on the 1947 trip to the "Little House" sites while preparing the 1953 editions. His generously offered use of the photographs taken in his travels greatly enhance the text, and give a fascinating look into the changes each site has undergone through the decades.

The cover illustration represents one of several pen-and-ink samples which Mr. Williams prepared for Harper and Brothers while considering the medium to be used in illustrating the new, uniform editions. This unpublished version of a *Little House in the Big Woods* scene was exhibited during the beloved illustrator's return to De Smet, South Dakota and Walnut Grove, Minnesota during the summer of 1986.

William Anderson,
Editor

Sixth Printing: 2000
Seventh Printing: 2005

INTRODUCTION

Generations of librarians, teachers, parents and book-sellers have regarded *The Horn Book Magazine* as an indispendable tool in their work. As a compass, the magazine directs the way to the very best in the world of children's books. As a rudder, it guides in creating vital reading experiences for the young.

It is natural that *Horn Book* has devoted many pages of its issues through the years to the works of Laura Ingalls Wilder. In fact, *Horn Book* immediately recognized the value of Laura's work-in-progress as she continued her saga following the publication of *Little House in the Big Woods* in 1932.

As interest in the "Little House" books accumulated following the publication of the last volume, *These Happy Golden Years* in 1943, *The Horn Book's* features on Laura Ingalls Wilder became definitive sources of supplemental information on the author and her work. Questioning "Little House" admirers, students preparing research papers and hundreds of children's literature classes were led to back issues of *The Horn Book* for additional glimpses of Laura.

Today, the tide of scholarship and its availability has turned. During the 1960's, 1970's and 1980's, a wide body of articles, lectures, reprints, and books has been published. Workshops, programs, colloquiums, conferences and college classes have helped to fill the gap in scholarship that once existed in Wilder studies.

It seems, however, that the earliest—and among the most excellent—sources of Laura Ingalls Wilder appreciation and enlightenment deserve to appear in print again. Hence, *The Horn Book's Laura Ingalls Wilder.*

The Horn Book first featured Laura Ingalls Wilder in a tribute by Irene Smith in the September, 1943 issue. Smith was Superintendent of Work with Children at the Brooklyn Public Library when she researched "Laura Ingalls Wilder and the Little House Books." The article was printed just after *These Happy Golden Years* was published with its final message: "The End of the Little House Books." That last-page pronouncement made morose readers; no one wanted to believe that there would be no more visits with Laura and Almanzo. But readers were assuaged by Irene Smith's splendid portrait of the Wilders which helped fill the gaps between 1885 and 1943 and left audiences with a satisfied feeling about the hero and heroine of the "Little Houses."

Smith's exclusive quotes from Laura and her daughter Rose Wilder Lane, her use of never-before-seen family pictures and her own appreciative prose resulted in a memorable tribute to the characters of the "Little House" books and their author.

The Smith article was incorporated into an issue with the theme of "Integrity and Idealism." In her editorial message, Bertha E. Mahoney prophesied the lasting, overwhelming world-wide impact and importance of Laura Ingalls Wilder's American saga . . .

It is particularly fitting that this should be the issue to carry Irene Smith's paper on Laura Ingalls Wilder and her books. There is a positive creative spirit in these books, embodying as they do the life of one American family, and already they are making their influence felt in the lives of many children . . . If our country can become great in humility, and can work earnestly to solve its own problems at the same time that it carries its share of world responsibilities, it will be through the vision of our children, their integrity and idealism, gained in homes like the home in the "Little House" books.

* * * * * * * *

Soon after the "Little House" books were complete in their eight-volume saga form, children's book editor Ursula Nordstrom at Harper and Brothers, investigated the possibility of a newly-illustrated, uniform sized edition of the Wilder books. Her first choice as illustrator was a newcomer to the field, Garth Williams. Williams' work on E.B. White's charming 1945 title, *Stuart Little,* had convinced Harpers that they very much wanted to keep the artist illustrating for them. Miss Nordstrom gave Mr. Williams a set of the Wilder books and told him to read the series.

Garth Williams was already established as a creator of fantastical talking animals; he wondered whether the realism of the "Little House" books was his forte. "When Ursula gave me the books to read, I looked through them to see if there were any spiders that talked, like *Charlotte's Web,* but they were very historical, very real. 'Do you think I'm the person to illustrate them?' I asked. 'I've only done animal books.' Miss Nordstrom said: 'You go home and read those books thoroughly and don't come back until you have.' I did and came back saying 'This is marvelous, and I'll do the illustrations!' "

Illustrating methods were discussed and debated. At one point, it was agreed that Garth would produce oil paintings depicting various seasonal scenes in the "Little House" books. But then came the message that the color would make the books prohibitive in price. Next, Garth submitted some pen-and-ink sketches (see sample on this book's cover). Finally, his soft pencil sketches were considered the best. Time has proved the superlative quality of this decision.

Garth Williams gives much credit for the final appearance to Helen Gentry, who designed the new editions. Her planning and foresight allowed Garth to do illustrations spreading over two pages, and she artistically planned each detail for the setting of his artistic work.

The "Little House" books were fortunate in having a dedicated illustrator who believed that the pictures to appear in the book should be as historically accurate as the text itself.

Garth Williams' first research took him out to Danbury, Connecticut, where he visited the Wilders' daughter Rose Wilder Lane in her King Street farmhouse. Garth hoped to visit with Laura, and he admitted that he mainly wanted to ascertain from Rose whether her mother's memory was clear and if she could receive guests. Rose assured Garth that indeed her parents were well and active and sharp-minded and that he must not hesitate visiting them in Mansfield, Missouri. She was also helpful in planning a trip route for the New Yorker who knew little of the lands west of the Hudson River. To see log cabins, Rose suggested that the Williams family drive through the Shenandoah Valley and out to Mansfield via the Smoky Mountains. From there, Garth Williams intended to visit each of the book-sites.

On the day in September 1947 when Garth drove up the lane and approached Rocky Ridge Farmhouse, Laura was weeding in the garden. "I sat and watched her," he remarked forty years later, and his impressions were still fresh and sharp. "I found her to be frisky, a person who seemed to be willing to try anything and go anywhere. She was a very cheerful character, very sprightly, very much alive with a very good sense of humor."

When Laura introduced the illustrator to Almanzo, who sat inside the house, all he could do was feel awe-struck. "There I stood, with the hero and heroine of the books," Garth marvelled. "What could be more exciting?"

Of their visit, one impression remained dominant to the illustrator of the "Little House" books: their author was unconcerned about the new drawings; she clearly thought that the text was predominate. As a result, she gave Garth free reign in his work. "I asked her," recalled the illustrator, 'Do you want me to draw portraits of you and your family? Or should I draw pleasant-appearing people to fit the story?' She said it didn't matter at all, so I said, 'I'll send you pictures before they are all finished and you can criticize them and I'll make changes.' She never asked for any changes!"

Most of the actual illustrating of the "Little House" books occurred while the Williams family resided in Italy. As illustrations arrived in New York City, editors at Harper and Brothers were increasingly excited about prospects for the new editions. As publication day neared in October, 1953, it was evident that a monumental project was soon to culminate.

News of the impending publication was regularly sent to Laura, who at 86 was still living in the white-painted farmhouse on Rocky Ridge. "Eight years is a long time, and I am now becoming a little impatient, but I expect to be well repaid for waiting when I see the Garth Williams illustrations in the new editions of my books," she wrote.

In July, 1953, when Laura received copies of the first four books of her series in their new format, she pronounced them "beautiful." And when she telegraphed her response to Harper and Brothers, all concerned with the publication of the new editions breathed a collective sign of satisfaction at the author's unqualified delight in the new versions of her books. "Mary, Laura and their folks live again in these illustrations," said Laura Ingalls Wilder.

Critics, librarians, educators and children all agreed that the marriage of the talents of Laura Ingalls Wilder and Garth Williams made the "Little House" books shine even brighter in their interpretation of life in the woods and on the prairies during the pioneer days. So enthusiastic was *The Horn Book Magazine* that their December, 1953 issue was devoted to the "Little House" books, their author and their new illustrator. "I am so pleased about it," wrote Laura. "There seems to be a great interest in the new edition and the Christmas Horn Book should add to it," she said.

Today, more than thirty years later, that same "great interest" still continues. It was exhibited wide-scale during the summer of 1986, when Garth Williams paid a nostalgic re-visit to the Wilder Country of Minnesota and South Dakota. In July, Garth was a guest of the Laura Ingalls Wilder Memorial Society in De Smet

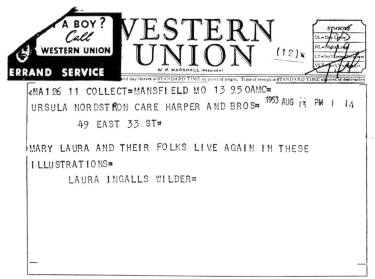

and the Laura Ingalls Wilder Museum of Walnut Grove.

During his visit, the sprightly artist re-traced his steps over the land where the Ingalls walked for the first time in 39 years. "Now it looks more civilized," he noted. "The trees are the most developed thing."

In both De Smet and Walnut Grove, long lines awaited the 74-year-old artist, as tourists and local residents flocked in to meet the man who, as author Barbara Walker says, "brought the sunshine into the 'Little House' books." Hundreds of books were autographed, and between visiting, book-signing session and touring the sites, Garth presented lectures on his life and his experiences illustrating the Wilder books.

"I was impressed with the way Laura saw the world through rosy glasses," Garth said. "She saw the beauty of everything simple . . ."

Year after year, generation after generation, readers share in that beauty Laura Ingalls Wilder wrote about and which Garth Williams depicted in illustrations.

The Horn Book's Laura Ingalls Wilder explains some of the story that resulted in the classic "Little House" books.

W.T.A.
April, 1987

Laura at 84 (1951).

LAURA INGALLS WILDER
AND THE LITTLE HOUSE BOOKS

By IRENE SMITH

L ATE last winter when cold weather was biding past its time, there came from Harper's a package of important content, as eagerly awaited as a spring day. Joyful welcomes rose to meet it in every library and bookstore where children's books are known. Many thousands of readers of all ages had been asking impatiently for this next Little House book. In it Laura was expected to marry Almanzo. Every one longed for one more reunion with the Ingalls family, Pa and Ma and the girls.

These Happy Golden Years was well worth the anticipation. Pleasure, however, was tinged with the gloom of goodbye, for the author said there would be no more Little House books. The story had ended.

This eighth volume closed in unaltered triumph one of the phenomenal achievements in modern literature for children, a genuine chronicle of American life and of family life at their equal best. Through these books young Laura Ingalls of the 1870's and '80's had stepped from pages of the past into the flesh and blood reality of a chosen friend. Today it is our privilege to salute this selfsame Laura, who at seventy-six is our most living heroine.

Laura Ingalls Wilder produced her first book, *Little House in the Big Woods,* in 1932. It told the story of log cabin life in the Big Woods of Wisconsin sixty years before. Readers recognized with delight that it was about real people. Pa and Ma, elder sister Mary (who later became blind), and little Carrie, the baby, were Laura's own family. The good bread Ma baked on Saturdays and the songs Pa played on his fiddle had nourished a child of that frontier day, creating an adult whose mind was stocked with living memories. These, set down late in her life, made a story which children of today immediately accepted for its truth and appeal. They gladly identified themselves with that long-ago family, and followed their homesteading trail plainly enchanted by the simplicity and sincerity of Mrs. Wilder's writing.

Charles and Caroline Ingalls moved west when they were married, first to Wisconsin where Mary, Laura, and Carrie were born.

The Ingalls family in 1891. Ma, Pa, and Mary seated. Carrie beside Ma. Laura with hand on Pa's shoulder. Grace. (Laura had been married six years when this was made.)

10

Laura was still small when they loaded their possessions into a covered wagon and moved to Indian Territory, now the plains of Kansas. *Little House on the Prairie* tells first about that trip, then about the year spent in the new cabin built by Pa. Ma thought he had done a good job, but Pa wished they had glass for the windows. Laura was proudly confident of the home's security against wolves.

They were all happy that night. The fire on the hearth was pleasant, for on the High Prairie even the summer nights were cool. The red-checked cloth was on the table, the little china woman glimmered on the mantel-shelf, and the new floor was golden in the flickering firelight. Outside, the night was large and full of stars. Pa sat for a long time in the doorway and played his fiddle and sang to Ma and Mary and Laura in the house and to the starry night outside.

Across Kansas, across Missouri, across Iowa the wagon again moved them the following autumn to another homestead, this time in Minnesota. One winter in a sod house, and then the comfortable new home with real windowpanes and a wonderful stove are the setting for *On the Banks of Plum Creek*. Laura was growing ruggedly. Helping Pa with his work as well as Ma with hers, playing with Mary and watching after Carrie, absorbing everything that happened, she never thought of their solitary lives as lacking in eventfulness. Yet most of the time they had only themselves, with few outside resources to supply variety.

Meantime, on a big farm in New York State belonging to the Wilder family, a boy ten years older than Laura was training his first team of oxen and earning for himself a beautiful colt named Starlight. Mrs. Wilder tells about Almanzo Wilder's boyhood in *Farmer Boy*, one of the most popular of her stories. Readers felt personally gratified when he reappeared in the next volume, as a young Dakota pioneer.

Charles Ingalls was a man of the outdoors, a farmer, hunter, and woodsman. After one more long move the Ingalls family settled in Dakota Territory, where Pa worked for the railroad until they took up their claim near Silver Lake. He built the first house on the new townsite, not far from the homestead described in *By the Shores of Silver Lake*, and took a leading part in the founding of DeSmet, South Dakota.

The last three are full-length books of close continuity and mounting dramatic interest, *The Long Winter, Little Town on the Prairie*, and *These Happy Golden Years*. Winters were spent in town after the hard one of 1880-81, when blizzards isolated the new settlement and Almanzo Wilder rode through terrible snows to bring back sorely needed wheat. There was a fourth Ingalls girl now, named Grace. Ma and Laura enjoyed the beginnings of social life in the town, but summers were best out on the Silver Lake homesite. Mary longed to go to college, and Laura joined whole-heartedly in the family sacrifices that finally made it possible. During this time Laura was getting her own education. At fifteen she held her teacher's certificate, and was riding with Almanzo behind his dashing team of horses. She taught for a year at a small school twelve miles from home, where she proved by her endurance of unspeakably miserable living quarters that, in the beloved surroundings of her own home, she had grown a valiant spirit and a vertical spine. Fortunately for the young schoolteacher, all the rigors of that Dakota winter failed to daunt Almanzo and his horses. Promptly after school on Friday his sleigh was at the door to rescue Laura from a homesick weekend. Their marriage and their own little house bring the happy conclusion satisfactory to every reader.

The essence of feeling toward Mrs. Wilder is gratitude, that she persevered in the telling of this long story, that she told it with such warmth and grace, and that the finished cycle will remain, to our lasting enrichment. If any words of tribute in these *Horn Book* pages could serve the wishes of children and of those elders who share their book enthusiasms, the words would form themselves into a wreath of affection and admiration, to hail Laura Ingalls Wilder for her achievement.

It is interesting to know that all this personal history was written first as matter-of-fact autobiography. Luckily for us it failed to reach publication. Later it was amplified and retold for children, beginning with a style appealing to the eight-year-olds and continuing in volumes of increasing length and difficulty. This graduation is a distinguishing feature of the Little House books. They have kept pace with the growing reader, right up to the teen-aged girls whose present reading of *These Happy Golden Years* is delightful in its intimacy, because they and Laura were small together.

Mrs. Wilder drafts her stories in big rough school-tablets, writing with pencil on both sides of the page. "That's the Scotch plus the hungry pioneer; she doesn't waste an inch of the cheapest paper." With several of these tablets filled she goes over and over the job, writing fresh bits in other tablets, cutting from the original and pinning in the new parts. She draws her own maps of the places concerned, so that her scenic descriptions are always accurate in their accompaniment of remembered events. Her books have been fortunate in their illustrators, Helen Sewell and Mildred Boyle.

Young Almanzo Wilder

The Laura of today is still pretty, " still quicker than a flash," and as Pa said once, when she had worked beside him in the field, " as strong as a little French horse." Her daughter, Rose Wilder Lane, gives us this vivid sketch: " She's the serious, wide-eyed girl now almost shyly hidden under a surface quickness and sparkle. She's little, about five feet tall; has very small hands and feet, and large violet-blue eyes; I have seen them purple. Baby-fine, pure white hair. She wears it short and well-groomed, and moves and speaks quickly, sometimes vivaciously. But her character is Scotch; she holds a purpose or opinion like granite. . . . She has a charming voice, with changing tones and colors in it, and is sometimes witty or fanciful, but this is always a little startling; she is never talkative and usually speaks in a matter-of-fact way. Often she is silent nearly all day long; she is completely self-reliant, is never lonely, has no need of companionship. She speaks only when she has something to say." (Mrs. Lane was born in that "little gray house in the west," described in the last pages of *These Happy Golden Years,* less than two years after the printed story closes. She was named for the prairie roses her father and mother gathered when they went driving in their buggy on Sunday afternoons.)

Rolling hill country near Mansfield, Missouri, has been the home of Laura and Almanzo Wilder since they moved in a cov-

Baby Grace

ered wagon from South Dakota in 1894. Their original purchase was, Mrs. Wilder tells us, "a rough forty acres of land, with five acres cleared of timber and a one-room log house, where the only way for light to enter with the door shut was through cracks between logs where the clinking had fallen out. Another little house." They had seen hard times since their marriage, which shortly preceded the beginning of the seven-year drought in the Dust Bowl. Almanzo's prosperity in the eighties enabled him to survive seven years of total crop failure, but this long disaster was of course followed by the panic of 1893. In 1891 the young couple had nearly died of diphtheria, their son did die, their house burned down, and Almanzo was left partially paralyzed. During his convalescence Laura worked twelve hours a day in a dressmaker's shop for a dollar in wages. The one hundred dollars she accumulated bought their new land in Missouri, which they named Rocky Ridge Farm.

During the years Rocky Ridge Farm has been enlarged to two hundred acres, cleared except for woodlots left to furnish firewood and fenceposts. Jersey cows and Leghorn hens have been its special pride. The ten-room farmhouse stands on top of a gently sloping knoll, surrounded by centuries-old oaks. " The slope in spring is so covered with wild hens-foot violets that at a distance it looks blue." Mrs. Wilder prefers wild flowers to cultivated ones and " Missouri is always a mass of wild flowers; the knoll changes colors all summer." Rocky Ridge Farm house was built of materials off its own land, oak for the frame, paneling, beams, and stairs; enormous rocks for the fireplace and chimney. The large living room is entirely paneled in oak, and so is the library.

The Wilders' first triumph in Missouri was the one-room frame house to which they moved after some years in the log cabin. That frame house remains as the farm kitchen, completely modern and electrified. Next to it are the dining room with screened dining-and-sitting porch, the large south bedroom and bath, and Mrs. Wilder's " office," in which she wrote the Little House books. In that same small office she handled a million dollars in federal loans to Ozark farmers, as secretary of the Mansfield Farm Loan Association, which she organized. She is a poultry expert, and articles on breeds of chickens and many other rural topics have issued from that office. She is an excellent cook and housekeeper, without being really fond of either duty.

Mrs. Wilder cooks their seven o'clock breakfast while her husband cares for their four milk goats and two calves. " Then he works in the garden or the shop where he loves to tinker while I do up the housework and go down the hill to the mail-box for the mail. I take our big brown and white spotted bulldog with me and we go for a half mile walk before we come back. After that the day is always full, for I do all my own work, and to care for a ten-room house is no small job. Besides the cooking and baking there is churning to do. I make all our own butter from cream off the goat milk.

"And when the day is over and evening comes we read our papers and magazines or play a game of cribbage. If we want music we turn on the radio. . . . "

Any one who read *Farmer Boy* could have offered the comfortable prediction that small Almanzo would live long and robustly. The food he enjoyed from his mother's ample kitchen has made his story a mouth-watering adventure for modern children, especially those who live in cities.

He felt a little better when he sat down to the good Sunday dinner. Mother sliced the hot rye'n'injun bread on the bread-board by her plate. Father's spoon cut deep into the chicken pie; he scooped out big pieces of thick crust and turned up their fluffy yellow undersides on the plate. He poured gravy over them; he dipped up big pieces of tender chicken, dark meat and white meat sliding from the bones. He added a mound of baked beans and topped it with a quivering slice of fat pork. At the edge of the plate he piled dark red beet pickles. And he handed the plate to Almanzo.

Silently Almanzo ate it all. Then he ate a piece of pumpkin pie, and he felt very full inside. But he ate a piece of apple pie with cheese.

That was Sunday. On any week day:

Almanzo went on eating. He was listening, but he was tasting the good taste of roast pork and apple sauce in every corner of his mouth. He took a long, cold drink of milk, and then he sighed and tucked his napkin farther in, and he reached for his pumpkin pie.

He cut off the quivering point of golden brown pumpkin, dark with spices and sugar. It melted on his tongue, and all his mouth and nose were spicy.

That same youngest Wilder is eighty-six now. His hair is not yet gray and he wears glasses only to read fine print. Although he cannot get automobile insurance because of his age, he drives the Chrysler car, with Mrs. Wilder sitting beside him " to backseat drive so he can enjoy the landscape without any worry." Just before the war they drove to Dakota.

The Wilders have been farmers since King John's time in England, and since 1632 in this country. " Like most sensible American farmers, my father was doing contour plowing, stopping erosion and practicing soil conservation when he was a boy in northern New York State, and has done so ever since," says Rose Wilder Lane. " My mother and father know every bird that comes onto the farm; they permit no hunting even of rabbits, and feed the quails through hard winters. During an icestorm my father walks over the whole place, putting grain out for the wild birds."

Readers inevitably want to know what happened to the rest

Hearthside at Rocky Ridge Farmhouse

of Laura's family. She tells us that Mary graduated from the Iowa College for the Blind in 1889. " In the graduating exercises on June 10th, Mary read an essay, ' Bide a Wee and Dinna Weary,' which showed the influence of Pa's old Scots songs. After her graduation, Mary lived happily at home with her music, and her raised print and Braille books. She knitted and sewed and took part in the housework."

Carrie and Grace Ingalls remained in South Dakota after they married. Carrie and Laura are now the only living members of the family. Carrie, a widow, still lives at Keystone, near the foot of Mount Rushmore in the Black Hills, famous for the presidential sculptures.

Mrs. Wilder ties three other story threads to satisfy our interest: " I never saw Nellie Oleson after she went east to New York as told in *Golden Years*. I heard some years later that she married and went with her husband to Washington State. . . . Cap Garland went his carefree, happy way for five years after Almanzo married. He was killed in an explosion of the boiler of a steam threshing machine. . . . Miss Wilder married and lived in Louisiana where she is buried. Almanzo is the only one of his immediate family now living."

Besides the Little House books, Laura Ingalls Wilder's only

other authorship has been devoted to magazine articles, which are usually of factual nature. Her writing for children therefore has mined freely in the long rich veins of her memory, which had reached full maturity before they were uncovered. Their discovery has gained far-reaching influence, and all of the influence is right, and honest, and worthy of the need that it satisfies. Mrs. Wilder's work is sound because the living it reflects was sound, and because it deals with fundamental elements of life which are deeply rooted in American hearts.

When one thinks back upon the eight Little House books the first of these elements to spring to mind is courage, the many-sided courage a family set between itself and the uncertain wilderness, where dangers too were many-sided, and sharpened always by the solitude. Pa's courage was a man's fearless kind, a shield for his womenfolks against every threat of trouble; with an unused plenty brimming in his merriment and his music.

The wind was screaming fiercer and louder outside. Snow whirled swish-swishing against the windows. But Pa's fiddle sang in the warm, lamp-lighted house.

Ma's courage was gentle and calm on its surface, and its bedrock was granite. She instilled it into her children by her example of unfailing equilibrium. The girls were bred to self-control and good behavior. Indians, wolves, the grasshopper plague, and hunger itself had tried their mettle before the frontier relented. Worst of all was the Hard Winter.

All winter long they had been crowded in the little kitchen, cold and hungry and working hard in the dark and the cold to twist enough hay to keep the fire going and to grind wheat in the coffee mill for the day's bread.

All that long, long winter, the only hope had been that sometime winter must end, sometime blizzards must stop, the sun would shine warm again and they could all get away from the town and go back to the homestead claim.

Now it was springtime. The Dakota prairie lay so warm and bright under the shining sun that it did not seem possible that it had ever been swept by the winds and snows of that hard winter. How wonderful it was, to be on the claim again! Laura wanted nothing more than just being outdoors. She felt she never could get enough sunshine soaked into her bones.

          ✻   ✻   ✻

The day was ending in perfect satisfaction. They were all there together. All the work, except the supper dishes, was done until tomorrow.

They were all enjoying good bread and butter, fried potatoes, cottage cheese, and lettuce leaves sprinkled with vinegar and sugar.

Beyond the open door and window the prairie was dusky but the sky was still pale, with the first stars beginning to quiver in it. The wind went by, and in the house the air stirred, pleasantly warmed by the cookstove and scented with prairie freshness and food and tea and a cleanness of soap and a faint lingering smell of the new boards that made the new bedrooms.

In all that satisfaction, perhaps the best part was knowing that tomorrow would be like today, the same and yet a little different from all other days, as this one had been.

Within their own walls there was complete security. They may have been the walls of a covered wagon, or a dugout, or an unroofed cabin, but there or in the finished house it was being together that mattered. This family solidarity was the stout fibre of the Ingallses, resistant to all wear. It made them strong when misfortunes struck them, and happy when the skies were blue, because nothing came to one alone and everything was shared by all. Fun-making rippled through their work and play, lightening their daily lives with homemade diversions, heartily enjoyed. They were indivisible, but it was a loyal, helpful unity, without self-righteousness. There was room for every friend and neighbor that needed kindness, or paused to share their spiritual bounty.

Incorruptible decency is the other characteristic element. In their lives it was innate. We find its outward expression in the fresh white curtains and the well-cooked meals, bravely defying the crude facilities of each new homestead. The firm moral principles, the respect and liking for work, the mutual consideration and unselfishness, came from the very tissues of their being.

In these books, then, that speak so eloquently of the courage that made our country big and free, of the family solidarity that is its cornerstone, and the decency that flames in its ideals, Laura Ingalls Wilder has recorded for all children an enduring, intrinsic story of America. It reminds a needy world today of the canniness of the pioneer, the strength and joy of the builder, and the dreams of free individuals working toward a better future. Young present-day readers can learn from Mrs. Wilder that vicissitudes must be faced, and that real happiness is not measured by material possessions. She enlarges and deepens their understanding of their native land when she tells them how it felt to live in a big woods, and on a raw new prairie homestead when frontiers were moving west. The waving fields of wheat and the summer blackberry thicket are the plentiful realization of good American earth. The carpenter's saw and the new muddy streets are proof of the frontier community built by families like the Ingallses. Where stores and houses sprang the church and school rose with them, bringing personal responsibilities of citizenship.

Laura attended the first Fourth of July celebration in the " little town on the prairie." Pa led the crowd in singing " My Country, 'Tis of Thee." The meaning of the occasion struck Laura with a completely new thought.

The Declaration and the song came together in her mind, and she thought: God is America's king. She thought: Americans won't obey any king on earth. Americans are free. That means they have to obey their own consciences. No king bosses Pa; he has to boss himself. Why (she thought), when I am a little older, Pa and Ma will stop telling me what to do, and there isn't anyone else who has a right to give me orders. I will have to make myself be good.

Underlying all this writing is the steadfast morality, felt in these reflective passages as the strong foundation upon which the story rests. The author's ideal of personal integrity was her father, whom she admired and adored. We are told that her deepest feeling about her own success is that now her father will not be entirely forgotten. She is giving his violin, an Amati, to the South Dakota Historical Museum, with a set of the

Mrs. Wilder as she is today with Rocky Ridge Farmhouse in the background

" *Come back soon, Laura* "

From "These Happy Golden Years," illustrated by
Mildred Boyle and Helen Sewell (Harper)

Little House books; a fitting memorial to a pioneer father and American citizen. Mrs. Wilder has written a verse in her daughter's copy of each finished book. The last inscription says:

> And so farewell to childhood days,
> Their joys, and hopes and fears.
> But Father's voice and his fiddle's song
> Go echoing down the years.

Thus is revealed the source of all her inspiration, from which has stemmed her beautifully written, honest, and unforgettable stories. The sheer power of Mrs. Wilder's memory has held the tie. Under its spell, voiding the distance back to childhood, she made her lasting magic:

Laura lay awake a little while, listening to Pa's fiddle softly playing and to the lonely sound of the wind in the Big Woods. She looked at Pa sitting on the bench by the hearth, the firelight gleaming on his brown hair and beard and glistening on the honey-brown fiddle. She looked at Ma, gently rocking and knitting.

She thought to herself, " This is now."

She was glad that the cosy house, and Pa and Ma and the firelight and the music, were now. They could not be forgotten, she thought, because now is now. It can never be a long time ago.

Pa's fiddle

OF BOOKS AND READING
FOR CHILDREN AND
YOUNG PEOPLE

T H E
Horn Book
MAGAZINE

December 1953

Laura Ingalls Wilder

ISSUE

A TRIBUTE TO
LAURA INGALLS WILDER

IT is with the greatest pleasure that *The Horn Book* here honors one of the most beloved of all children's authors and joins in the tribute paid to her by all the contributors to this Christmas issue. It is a tribute that will grow with every reader of the magazine; so that Christmas wishes will be flying to Mansfield, Missouri, from all over America and from countries beyond the seas. It is fitting that this should be so, for seldom have there been any children's books so universally loved.

Yet, I thought as I read Miss Dalphin's " Christmas in the Little House Books," and the letter from Germany on page 486 that there is more than one way of repaying in some measure the joy that the books about Laura and Mary have brought to children everywhere.

We read how the small Ingalls girls were made so happy by so little and we are apt to think that times have changed and that children today have much more. But then we are forgetting the boys and girls in war-torn countries who have even less than Laura and Mary had in material goods, and — in many cases — none at all of the love and security that enveloped them.

It was people like Pa and Ma with their high ideals and their practical industry and courage that made this country. If they were still alive they would feel deeply the responsibilities their America must now take in a wider world; and Laura and Mary would be taught to share all that they had.

Surely no tribute could please Mrs. Wilder more than that the children of 1953, remembering each Christmas they have enjoyed with Laura and Mary, should as a special thank-you share their own Christmas with children in countries less fortunate than ours; and thus help to keep alive in the world that thoughtful, friendly spirit which made it " Christmas all the time " in the Little House books.   J. D. L.

"Mr. Wilder came in . . ."   *Garth Williams*

"Mrs. Wilder was working in her garden . . ."

THE HORN BOOK

MAGAZINE

December, 1953

ILLUSTRATING
THE LITTLE HOUSE BOOKS

By GARTH WILLIAMS

WHEN Ursula Nordstrom asked me to illustrate the new edition of the Laura Ingalls Wilder books I wanted very much to do so. I loved and admired the books myself and they had meant a great deal to my small daughters when we read them aloud together. But my knowledge of the West at that time was almost zero and I could not see myself undertaking the work happily until I had seen the country that formed the background of the stories. And so I decided to visit Mrs. Wilder in Mansfield, Missouri, where she still lives; and then follow the route which the Ingalls family took in their covered wagon.

I was spending the summer with my family on a very primitive farm in New York State. We had neither telephone nor electricity. The house had five barns and a smokehouse. Our water came down from a crystal-clear spring in the woods, and our only mechanical convenience was a hand-pump in the kitchen, located in a lean-to with a very leaky roof. We were situated on a high hill surrounded by two hundred acres. The house was almost two hundred years old and the main barn was a giant, built when the farmers vied with one another to build the largest. Three years earlier the farm was still being run by the old couple who had lived there for eighty years exactly in the manner of the Wilders in Malone, New York, as described in *Farmer Boy*. It was not surprising then to find as I studied the books that time seemed to slip back seventy or eighty years. I had to clean lamps and trim wicks and I would place little bits of decorative red flannel in the glass bowls of the lamps as Caroline Ingalls had done in the book I had just put down.

Early in September we set out by car, drove through the Smokies and reached Mansfield, Missouri, ten days later. Mrs. Wilder was working in her garden when we arrived and was without any doubt the Laura of her books. She was small and nimble. Her eyes sparkled with good humor and she seemed a good twenty years younger than her age.

She took us into the house and we looked at all her old family photographs. She told us about the people and just where to find Plum Creek and the other places mentioned in the books. Mr. Almanzo Wilder came in and we talked of his youth in Malone, New York. I asked about many things and of course particularly about Pa's fiddle.

Mrs. Wilder told us that it is now kept in a museum in Pierre, South Dakota, and once every year it is taken out of its exhibit case and someone plays on it the songs Pa used to play for Laura and Mary. Some years ago Mrs. Wilder sent it to New York for a book exhibition. In the same package was the calico quilt which Mary made just after she became blind. Everyone was shocked to find that the package had not been insured, especially as the violin proved to be an extremely valuable Amati!

When I said that we were about to go down to the site of *Little House on the Prairie* on the Verdigris River in Oklahoma, and then from there to Plum Creek in Minnesota and on to De Smet, South Dakota, Mr. Wilder was worried because heavy snow was reported to be falling in the Rockies.

" Those blizzards can blow for weeks; I don't think you should risk going to De Smet at that time of year."

But Mrs. Wilder said very characteristically, "Oh, *I* would go!"

Two days later I was in Oklahoma following a dirt wagon road along the Verdigris River. As I rounded a bend I met an elderly man driving a two-horse wagon. I stopped to speak to him and asked if he knew anything of the Ingalls family. He told me that

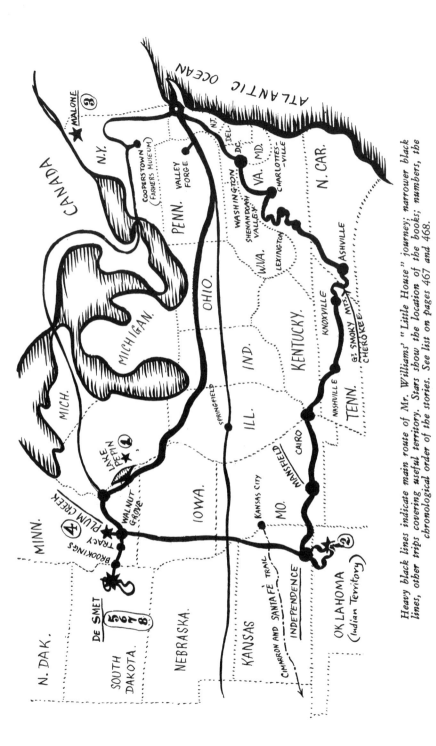

Heavy black lines indicate main route of Mr. Williams' "Little House" journey; narrower black lines, other trips covering useful territory. Stars show the location of the books; numbers, the chronological order of the stories. See list on pages 467 and 468.

ATLANTIC OCEAN

CANADA

MINN.
N. DAK.
SOUTH DAKOTA.
De SMET ⑤ ⑥ ⑦ ⑧
BROOKINGS
PLUM CREEK ④
TRACY
WALNUT GROVE
LAKE PEPIN ①
MICH.
MICHIGAN.
IOWA.
NEBRASKA.
KANSAS
KANSAS CITY
INDEPENDENCE
CIMARRON AND SANTA FÉ TRAIL
OKLAHOMA (Indian Territory) ②
MO.
MANSFIELD
CAIRO
ILL.
IND.
SPRINGFIELD
OHIO.
NASHVILLE
TENN.
KNOXVILLE
GT. SMOKY MTS.
CHEROKEE
KENTUCKY.
ASHVILLE
N. CAR.
LEXINGTON
W.VA.
SHENANDOAH VALLEY
VA.
CHARLOTTESVILLE
MD.
D.C.
WASHINGTON
DEL.
N.J.
PENN.
VALLEY FORGE
COOPERSTOWN (FARMERS MUSEUM)
N.Y.
MALONE ③

29

he had arrived in the vicinity when he was a boy and could recall the people that took over the little house on the prairie after the Ingalls family left. The house had now gone but at least I could see where it used to stand.

We drove to Independence, Kansas, following as closely as possible the route taken by Pa. I stood on the banks of the Verdigris River at the place where Mr. Edwards swam across that cold December day in 1873 just so that he could bring Christmas to " two little young girls named Mary and Laura." And I thought of that day in the little house on the prairie when the creek rose so high that " they knew they would have no Christmas, because Santa Claus could not cross that roaring creek." And they were all sad — Pa, Ma and Laura and Mary. And Ma was worried not only about Santa Claus. She also " hated to think of Mr. Edwards eating his bachelor cooking alone on Christmas Day. Mr. Edwards had been asked to eat Christmas dinner with them, but Pa shook his head and said a man would risk his neck, trying to cross that creek now."

And that was just what Mr. Edwards had done. He had risked his neck right here in this river and carried Santa Claus's presents with him so that two little girls could have Christmas.

I went back to the car and we drove on to Walnut Grove, Minnesota, and I could imagine myself as Pa Ingalls in a covered wagon creeping slowly across the vast prairie.

At the offices of *The Walnut Grove Tribune,* Mr. Lantz, the editor, was surprised to learn that *their* Plum Creek was the one Mrs. Wilder was writing about. But in *A Half Century of Progress,* published by the paper in 1916, we found Pa's name:

". . . The people living within the vicinity of the station petitioned to be set apart as an independent Village, and on March 13, 1879, held their first election resulting in the following officials being elected:

" President, Elias Bedal; Justice, Charles Ingalls. . . ."

A Golden Anniversary Edition of *The Walnut Grove Tribune* given me by Mr. Lantz provided me with many early pictures of the town and people.

He directed me to Plum Creek, which I followed on a very muddy cart track until I reached a farmhouse on the bank. The grandparents living in the house remembered many of the characters in the book *On the Banks of Plum Creek* but nothing of a sod house in the bank, although, according to Mrs. Wilder's

Plum Creek

The Verdigris River in Kansas, as photographed by Garth Williams in 1947.

description, it could not have been more than a quarter of a mile from their place. I left the car in their yard and followed the stream, taking my camera with me. I did not expect to find the house, but I felt certain that it would have left an indentation in the bank. A light rain did not help my search and I was just about to give up when ahead of me I saw exactly what I was looking for, a hollow in the East Bank of Plum Creek. I felt very well rewarded, for the scene fitted Mrs. Wilder's description perfectly. I took my pictures and returned to Walnut Grove and we drove on to Tracy and then to De Smet, the scene of the last four books.

Next morning I went to *The De Smet News* and Mr. Sherwood, the publisher, took me to the shores of Silver Lake and showed me where Pa Ingalls put up their claim shanty. Then he drove me all over town, pointing out the old places and giving me also the history that followed after the last of Mrs. Wilder's books. Pa and Ma remained in De Smet to the end of their lives. Carrie became Mrs. D. N. Swanzey. Grace became Mrs. Nate Dow and

Garth's photo of the Ingalls homestead site in De Smet.

lived in a small town nearby, to the west, called Manchester. Mary never married.

Mr. Sherwood gave me the Fiftieth Anniversary Edition of *The De Smet News* of June 6, 1930, and in it I found many references to the characters in the books and to the Hard Winter of 1880. Here are a few:

"Ingalls was first resident of De Smet. He was the first resident, first to have a family with him here, quite possibly first to establish a home on the townsite, first justice of the peace and first town clerk."

"The Ingalls home was a stopping place for the early home-seekers, and they played host as best they could, their house being practically a hotel that first year."

"Another early school was the Bouchie school and the early teacher was Laura Ingalls of De Smet."

"The first religious service in the community was held in the Ingalls home near Silver Lake on February 29, 1880."

"Arriving back here about April 20, 1880, to build his shanty and state residence on his land, Mr. Dow found the beginning of De Smet. He was surprised to see a shanty on his land and at first thought someone had jumped his claim, but found it to be the railroad house, with the Ingalls family living in it. This was moved to De Smet, standing to-day near the entrance to the ball park."

"The first public school of several grades was presided over by Mrs. C. L. Dawley, nee Florence Garland. Miss Garland received a salary of $20.00 per month for teaching the dozen pupils. She was followed by Miss Wilder [Almanzo's sister]. . . . Miss Wilder taught during the school year of 1881 and 1882."

"The square in which the Congregational church stood was used as a pasture for cows, through which the children disliked to pass."

"The fall and early winter was fine and Christmas Day people from far and wide gathered at the Ingalls home for a picnic dinner. There were about seventy-five persons present; most of them were strangers, however, they quickly became acquainted and all had a happy time."

That Christmas Day was the beginning of the Hard Winter described by Mrs. Wilder in *The Long Winter*.

The house, south of Silver Lake, stood empty on the prairie and I wandered around it, peering into the windows where Laura, Pa, Ma, Mary, Carrie and Baby Grace once sat. The air was fresh and clear and the sky a quiet blue. I could imagine the children playing in the buffalo grass out on that vast prairie. I drove south over the muddy roads to where Laura taught school and where Almanzo came courting. Over the same rolling prairie that

Almanzo and Cap Garland sledded with the supply of wheat for the starving town in that winter of 1880.

I returned to the town and talked with Mrs. Sterr who had been a playmate of Carrie and Grace and heard her tell many stories of those early days. I talked with Mr. Masters who was a contemporary of Mrs. Wilder. He remembered every change in the town since those first claim shanties. " Those stories," he said, " are more than just stories for us. They are our lives, we lived them."

The Big Slough, with Ingalls claim on the horizon, in November, 1947.

As the sun set we drove out of De Smet in the direction of Minnesota. The radio reported a heavy snowstorm thirty miles to the west. I thought of Mr. Wilder and drove fast into the dark. When we reached Sherburn, Minnesota, where we were going to stay with friends, a fierce cold wind began to blow and as we sat down to dinner a swirling snow enveloped the house; but I had seen the background of the Little House books. Seen the land, the houses and many of the people.

As my own farm was in the same state and territory as the Wilders' of Malone, all I required for *Farmer Boy* were pictures of the town of that day. A letter of mine was thoughtfully sent

Pastel by Almanzo Wilder's Aunt, Sarah Wilder Day.

to a local paper by Mr. Dumas, the acting postmaster, and the people there were most kind and many lent me early photographs and drawings. These included pictures of the church, the Wilder house, the Franklin School, the early streets and the memorial park. This account would be incomplete if I omitted to mention the help given me by Mr. Clarence Dumas, Mr. V. B. Roby, Mrs. M. P. House, Mrs. F. E. Smith, granddaughter of Sarah Wilder, and Mr. Clarence E. Kilburn whose letter from Mrs. Wilder appears elsewhere in this issue.

With costumes and the early pioneer equipment and methods of living I was given great assistance by the Farmer's Museum of Cooperstown, New York. Among the many interesting things I found there was a stoneware jug with the name Ingalls on it.

Yet even with all the data I collected it must not be assumed that every character is a portrait or that every detail is accurate. With the limited space for illustrations I could only dip into the large amount of information available and use what seemed most important.

Illustrating books is not just making pictures of the houses, the people and the articles mentioned by the author; the artist has to see everything with the same eyes. For example, an architect would have described the sod house on the bank of Plum Creek as extremely primitive, unhealthy and undesirable — nothing to seal the walls from dampness, no ventilation, no light. But to Laura's fresh young eyes it was a pleasant house, surrounded by flowers and with the music of a running stream and rustling leaves.

She understood the meaning of hardship and struggle, of joy and work, of shyness and bravery. She was never overcome by drabness or squalor. She never glamorized anything; yet she saw the loveliness in everything. This was the way the illustrator had to follow — no glamorizing for him either; no giving everyone a permanent wave.

It is now ten years since I began to try to recreate in pictures the lives of Laura and Mary. It has been for me a most exciting adventure.

Garth and the Ingalls homestead site, De Smet

Photo by N. D. Potter

Garth Williams at 80 (1992)

THE DISCOVERY OF
LAURA INGALLS WILDER

By Virginia Kirkus

I AM sure Mrs. Wilder would be astonished to learn that she needed to be " discovered " back in 1931. For she began discovering herself at a very early age and the years since 1931 have proved that nothing of her own early years had been lost. But there was a very real sense of discovery on my part as I began reading the manuscript of *Little House in the Big Woods* on a late-afternoon train bound for Westport, Connecticut. To be sure, I had already missed one train, while I had the first whispers poured into my eager ears; and I went one stop beyond my station on the late train, so absorbed was I in learning to know small Laura, as her little-girl days were re-lived in her story.

How did that manuscript come into my hands? Well, it is an odd story and one that cannot all be told. But it started with a mysterious telephone conversation with an acquaintance who had seen the manuscript and thought I might be interested. Those were the days when children's books were coming into their own. Louise Seaman at Macmillan, May Massee at Doubleday, Bertha Gunterman at Longmans, Helen Fish at Stokes and I at Harpers were doing considerable trail blazing in a field that had long been fairly static. But the " depression " was making its impress on our sales; people were thinking that new books for children were unnecessary, while the old ones could serve. And all of us were hoping for that miracle book that no depression could stop.

What I was told on the phone about the manuscript failed to spark my interest. "An elderly lady was writing a true story — in fictional form — about her pioneer childhood." Well, I'd heard that tale before; but, yes, I could meet my friend for a spot of tea at the Biltmore, just before train time. And then I heard more, and my own well-remembered love for stories from my grandmother about " when she was a little girl " made me decide to read the manuscript and give a " yes " or " no " by phone before Monday. There were reasons which one need not go into here for the necessity of a quick decision. And the reasons why that decision was an emphatic " Yes " lay in the manuscript itself.

At that time I was living a fairly rugged life in a house lighted with kerosene lamps — a house with only the most elementary plumbing, a kitchen pump. Perhaps that was one reason why I was so quickly translated to those Wisconsin woods and small Laura's adventures. But the real magic was in the telling. One felt that one was listening, not reading. And picture after picture — still vivid today, more than twenty years later — flashed before my inward eye. I knew Laura — and the older Laura who was telling her story. Here was the book no depression could stop — and here was, I felt sure, the beginning of a continued story for the years to follow.

And so *Little House in the Big Woods* and its creator, Laura Ingalls Wilder, were " discovered." And a book friendship formed. I did not then know that her daughter was Rose Wilder Lane. I did not know that the story of the successive moves of the Ingalls family would build up a contemporary children's classic. But I did know that Harpers wanted to publish Laura Ingalls Wilder and wanted to see more and hear more about her.

Although I left Harpers while the second book, *Little House on the Prairie,* was still in the making, I had a finger in the pie,

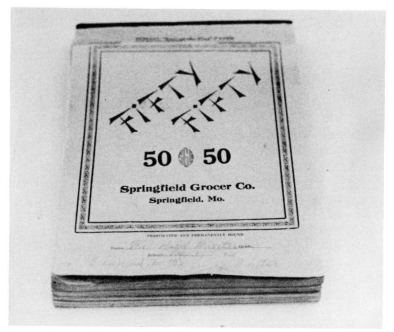

One of Laura's manuscripts.

then and in the books to come. They met a demand that has not flagged in the years. Witness the worn condition of the books in every public library. Children like to grow up with their central character and to share the " lived-happily-ever-after " years. And children love the sense of identification these books give. My grandniece is deep in them now, — at ten sharing them by reading them aloud to her younger brother and sister; for these are perfect family books and their savor does not dim. I look back on the " discovery " of Laura Ingalls Wilder as one of the milestones in my life with books — one of the rewards I still enjoy.

The new edition has just been published and we have had a preview at our little country library in Connecticut. The children are ecstatic over the gay jackets, and pore over the sketches with their lively quality of adventure and humor and their decorative, period feel. I loved the original Helen Sewell drawings, but the jackets lacked " pull " and the books, as they came along, were uneven in picture quality. Now — with the Garth Williams pictures, there is a sense of growing up with the stories, as Laura herself grows up. A new generation of readers will claim them as their own. They, too, will have a part in the sense of discovery.

CHRISTMAS
IN THE LITTLE HOUSE BOOKS

By Marcia Dalphin

ONE DAY Mrs. Ingalls and her two little daughters were talking about Christmas and Santa Claus. " ' If everybody wanted everybody else to be happy, all the time, then would it be Christmas all the time? ' Laura asked, and Ma said, ' Yes, Laura.' "

As I re-read all the Little House books recently, one right after the other, swiftly but attentively, I thought that if happiness is the touchstone, it really *was* Christmas all the time in the Ingalls home, and this despite everything. And when I say everything I mean it! I mean that in spite of this pioneer family's precarious economic situation, with a lack of this world's goods that would to many of us seem an impossible handicap; and in spite of the experience of coming up against the direst manifestations of Nature — grasshopper plagues, blizzards, prairie fires, cyclones, and much else in the way of unexpected accidents and near-disasters; in spite of all this, always in these books we are given a sense of the deep contentment and security that the children felt in their home. It did not matter that the home might be only a sod house under the creek bank, a roofless shack or merely the covered wagon stopping on the prairie for the night.

It was, of course, the warm, all-enveloping love of Pa and Ma for each other and for their children that made this so. Ma surpassed any woman I have ever known in the hardships she would accept to make her husband happy. How could this natural homemaker, with a love for pretty things and a longing for stability, take in her stride the incessant pulling-up of stakes that Pa's itching, west-wandering foot imposed upon her? It was always, "Whatever you say, Charles! " Truly these pioneer women were wonderful!

There is at least one Christmas chapter in each of the eight books; sometimes there are two. What else would one expect in a chronicle which gives us through its wealth of detail such a sense of the continuity of life, of season following season? It is hardly possible to pick a favorite among them.

Some might choose the first, in the little house in the big woods of Wisconsin when Laura and Mary were small. That was the year when Ma's present was the wall bracket that Pa whittled out for her little china woman to stand on; and when the stockings that Laura and Mary and their three visiting cousins hung up held only red mittens and one long stick of peppermint candy for each child. Laura had also a rag doll that her mother had made, but the other children were not jealous, because she was the littlest. " They were all so happy they could hardly speak at first. They just looked with shining eyes at those lovely Christmas presents."

Yet, it was not their gifts alone which made Christmas the happy day it was. It was made up of so many things: the preparations for the arrival of Uncle Peter, Aunt Eliza and the cousins; the baking of rye'n'Injun bread and Swedish crackers and vinegar pies and dried apple pies; the big bobsled coming through the snowy woods with sleigh bells jingling; the excitement of sleeping four in a row in a bed made on the floor; the pancake men for breakfast; the fun in the snow; the good dinner.

And that was the Christmas when Laura, lying wakeful, heard Uncle Peter telling how Prince saved Aunt Eliza from the panther. This is one of the scenes which, with many others in Mrs. Wilder's books, lingers in the memory. One can see so plainly the little girl lying in the improvised bed, watching the firelight flickering on the log wall, drowsily and contentedly listening to the voices of the older people as they sat talking by the fire. And, just as she is dropping off, hearing Uncle Peter say, " Eliza had a narrow squeak the other day, when I was at

Lake City. You know Prince, that big dog of mine? "

Sleep is a thing of the past until the story is told, and by that time the other children have waked and Ma finally tells Pa that to quiet them he will have to bring out his fiddle and play them to sleep. So Laura is lulled into slumber with " Money Musk " and " Nelly Gray." It is all so natural and simple and sweet.

Then there was that Christmas in *Little House on the Prairie* when there had been no snow and it had rained so long that the creek was in flood and the little girls knew that neither Santa Claus nor Mr. Edwards, the lonely neighbor who had been invited for dinner, would be able to cross it. But early on Christmas morning the door latch rattled and someone called, " Ingalls! Ingalls! " and there was Mr. Edwards, the red-haired, rangy Tennesseean. He had walked the forty miles from his cabin to Independence and back and swum the creek with his clothes on his head! And now, sitting on the floor by the children's bed, he gave them a most convincing, circumstantial account of how he had met Santa Claus in the street in Independence, and had been asked by him if he knew Mary and Laura Ingalls, and would he please do him the favor this once of fetching them their presents because he could not figure out any way whatsoever to get to their cabin with the water in the creek so high. While he was talking Ma had been busy, and when the girls next looked toward their stockings which had dangled so limply the night

before they seemed surprisingly lumpy. In each was a bright tin cup, a stick of candy and a little heart-shaped cake made with *white* flour and sprinkled with *white* sugar. And as if that were not enough, there was a new penny in the toe of each stocking! That was a day! And what a dinner, for Pa had shot a wild turkey and Mr. Edwards had brought nine sweet potatoes in his pockets, for ballast, he said, when he swam the creek.

Yet the Christmas that shines in my memory with a special radiance is that in *The Long Winter*. Up in Dakota, where Pa had at last proved his homestead claim, the Indians said (and the settlers found it true) that every seventh winter was a hard one, and at the end of three times seven came the hardest of all, with seven months of blizzards. Pa, for once, was apprehensive. On impulse they moved into the little nearby town, leaving for the winter the hastily built claim shanty; and scarcely had they settled when the first of the terrible, steadily recurring blizzards struck. This was in October. *The last one came in April.*

That year the trains stopped running, the food stores ran out of provisions entirely; in the end there was no coal, no wood, no kerosene. There was a long stretch when the only heat the Ingalls family had came from hay twisted into sticks by Pa and Laura, working with stiff, cold hands, day after day for hours and hours; when there was no more flour to make bread, just one sack of wheat which Pa had got with much difficulty. " ' It's a pity there isn't a grist mill in town,' Pa said. ' We have a mill,' Ma said. She reached to the top of the cupboard and took down the coffee mill." So they ground the wheat, a half-cupful at a time, and Ma made bread with it, and that was all they had to eat except potatoes, salt, a few turnips and tea. When the kerosene was gone, Ma made a lamp out of a button, a piece of calico and some axle grease.

You may wonder how any Christmas cheer was managed that winter, but if you think they threw in their hands, you are reckoning without Mrs. Ingalls and her daughters. Calling a council before Christmas, Ma made a suggestion. Someone had just sent them a bundle of *Youth's Companions*. Those they would save unopened so that they would have something to look forward to for Christmas Day. She said, " We can't spare money for presents, but we can have a happy Christmas just the same. I'll try to contrive something extra for dinner and then we'll open our papers and read them, and when it's too dark to read, Pa will play the fiddle."

After all, it was Pa who " contrived," for he managed to buy the last two cans of oysters on the store shelves and they had oyster soup (a great treat) and toasted bread for dinner. Even as they were eating it, down swept another terrible blizzard, blotting out the sunshine, the sky, the town. Still, all afternoon they had a lovely time reading aloud three stories from the hoarded papers. But that was the night the coal and the kerosene came to an end. The lamp flickered and went out just as they finished supper.

" ' The fire is dying anyway, so we may as well go to bed,' Ma said gently. Christmas Day was over."

Sincerely wishing you a very joyful Christmas and a year of happy days.

Laura Ingalls Wilder

A LETTER FROM
LAURA INGALLS WILDER

I T IS a long story, filled with sunshine and shadow, that we have lived since *These Happy Golden Years*.

In the first few years of our marriage we experienced complete destruction of our crops by hail storms; the loss of our little house by fire; the loss of Almanzo's health from a stroke of paralysis and then the drouth years of 1892-93-94.

In the fall of 1894 we, with our seven-year-old daughter, Rose, left Dakota by way of a covered wagon holding all our worldly goods, drawn by our team of horses. We arrived in Mansfield, Missouri, with enough money to make a part payment on a rough, rocky forty acres of land and a little left to buy our food for a time. The only building on the land was a one-room log cabin with a rock fireplace, one door but no window. When the door was closed light came in between the logs of the walls where the mud chinking had fallen out. We lived there a year.

Almanzo had recovered from the stroke but was not strong. He changed work with neighbors to build a log barn for his horses and a henhouse for a few hens.

In the spring we planted a garden and together we cleared land of timber. I never could use an ax but I could handle one end of a cross-cut saw and pile brush ready to burn. Almanzo made rails and stove wood out of the trees we cut down. With the rails he fenced the land we cleared; the stove wood he sold in town for 75¢ a wagon load with top box on. I hoed in the garden and tended my hens. We sold eggs and potatoes from our new-ground planting besides the wood and when we were able to buy a cow and a little pig we thought we were rich.

After that it was much easier. We worked and saved from year to year, adding to our land until we owned 200 acres well improved; a fine herd of cows; good hogs and the best laying flock of hens in the country.

These years were not all filled with work. Rose walked three-quarters of a mile to school the second year and after and her schoolmates visited her on Saturdays. She and I played along the little creek near the house. We tamed the wild birds and squirrels; picked wild flowers and berries. Almanzo and I often went horse-back riding over the hills and through the woods. And always we had our papers and books from the school library for reading in the evenings and on Sunday afternoons.

P.S. I cannot resist telling you that when we were building up our 200-acre farm we also built a 10-room farm house, using mostly material from the farm. We used hand-finished oak lumber from our own trees to panel rooms and build the open stairs, and hand-finished oak beams in the ceiling. At that time there was no planing mill to finish the lumber.

Laura's kitchen on Rocky Ridge Farm.

LAURA'S GINGERBREAD

Editor's Note: When we heard that Laura Ingalls Wilder is famous far and wide for her gingerbread, we thought what fun it would be for the thousands of children who love her books to make Laura's Gingerbread for Christmas. Consequently we wrote to Mrs. Wilder and she graciously sent us the recipe and wishes for good luck to all who try it!

> 1 cup brown sugar blended with
> ½ cup lard or other shortening.
> 1 cup molasses mixed well with this.
> 2 teaspoons baking soda in 1 cup boiling water
> (Be sure cup is full of water after foam is run
> off into cake mixture).
> Mix all well.

To 3 cups of flour have added one teaspoon each of the following spices: ginger, cinnamon, allspice, nutmeg, cloves; and ½ teaspoon salt. Sift all into cake mixture and mix well.

Add lastly 2 well-beaten eggs.

The mixture should be quite thin.

Bake in a moderate oven for thirty minutes.

Raisins and, or, candied fruit may be added and a chocolate frosting adds to the goodness.

GARTH WILLIAMS AFTER EIGHTY

By William Anderson

I certainly never started out to become a famous children's book illustrator," admits Garth Williams, whose art has decorated scores of notable books during the past half century. "But, looking back at my life, it appears I don't know there is anything else but drawing. I simply have this defect that I can draw. Others have it in music or mathematics; mine is art," says the man who estimates that he has illustrated ninety-seven books.

Garth Williams turned eighty in April of 1992, and though he can reflect on a laurel-filled career in children's illustration, he says he's far from finished with his work. The urge to draw and to yield to his lifelong creativity is still strong. "I find that as I get older, I remain the same as I was in my twenties and thirties; my tastes and interests haven't changed," he says. "I'm happiest when I'm busy drawing, and I think I should do three more books to make an even hundred that say 'Illustrated by Garth Williams.'"

The Williams family background was well suited to nurture Garth's artistic leanings. When he was born in New York City on April 16, 1912, both parents, Hamilton and Fiona Williams, were actively involved in the art world. Ham Williams illustrated for the British humor magazine *Punch*, and his wife was a Paris-trained painter. Their British background still colors their son's cultured, BBC-tinted voice, although his earliest memories are of a farm near Caldwell, New Jersey.

Garth Williams's first work of art was a stick-figured pine tree, drawn when he was nine months old. His father told him later that he reached his hand from a highchair to draw with one finger on a steamy kitchen window. "That settles it," his father declared. "He's going to be an artist." The prophecy held true: from that time to this, Garth Williams's life has been one of

Noted historian William Anderson is the author of Laura Ingalls Wilder Country, A Little House Sampler, *and* Laura Ingalls Wilder: A Biography *(Harper).*

almost unbroken activity in the creative arts – as a student, a teacher, a sculptor, painter, and illustrator.

His first ten years were spent in what he describes as a "Huckleberry Finn boyhood" in the countryside of New Jersey and Canada, experiences which later affected many of his illustrating assignments. For a while he was immersed in music; his sister gave him a ukulele for his eighth birthday. But his tastes later shifted to piano, classical guitar, tenor saxophone, and clarinet. "I learned the first movement of the *Moonlight Sonata* to impress the eight-year-old girl next door," he remembers today.

In 1922 the Williams family moved to England, where Garth was educated. He discovered that "at ten I could draw as well as any man." His skill landed him a job as an architect's assistant in London. He values that early training and the chances it gave him to crawl around the hidden recesses, domes, and niches of such famous spots as St. Paul's Cathedral.

By the time Williams was ready to enter architecture school, the Depression had slowed all construction in the British Isles and made a career as an architect impractical. Instead, he accepted his mother's offer of what she could afford – three months' tuition at Westminster Art School. Later, he was awarded a four-year scholarship to the Royal College of Art.

In 1936 Garth Williams won the British Prix de Rome for sculpture, an art form he says he still favors. He taught for a while, then lived a bohemian life traveling throughout Europe, painting and visiting galleries. He married the first of his four wives, realized that Hitler's menace would overrun Europe, and returned to London, where illustrators were in scant demand but war workers were greatly needed. He signed on with the Red Cross during the London Blitz and had some hair-raising experiences, including collecting the dead and injured from city streets and surviving a bomb blast which vaporized a friend walking next to him. "I realized," he says, "that I had a fifty-fifty chance of surviving the war."

Williams sent his wife and child to Canada and, at Churchill's suggestion, sailed to America, hoping to obtain a commission to do war work for Americans in Europe. The plan fell through; his letter from Churchill was considered a forgery. But this left the Williams family safe in the States for the duration. It also led Garth Williams back to the drawing boards in New York City.

The New Yorker started publishing Garth Williams's work, and then he illustrated an old English rhyme which was published as *The Chicken Book* (Delacorte). In 1945, he dropped off his portfo-

Illustration by Garth Williams from *Stuart Little.* © 1945 by E. B. White.

lio at the children's department at Harper and Brothers; coincidentally, E. B. White's *Stuart Little* manuscript arrived on Ursula Nordstrom's desk at the same time. When asked about his preference for an illustrator, White had remarked, "Try Garth Williams."

The illustrator tackled *Stuart Little* with gusto. The story of a mouse who became the son of a typical American family sparked for the first time the whimsical, fantasy-oriented Williams style. He says he found his muse in a real-life mouse who moved into the New York studio on the day he started the illustrating job.

Stuart Little established Garth Williams as a children's illustrator. It also showed his special affinity for depicting animals with particular sensitivity. "Some books are so wonderful that I would have illustrated them simply for the pleasure of it," he notes. This includes his second collaboration with E. B. White, *Charlotte's Web* (Harper). "It's one of my favorites," Williams says. "I feel lucky to share in any book that I love."

Always eagerly sought by authors as illustrator for their work, Garth Williams cites unusually creative chemistries with many important children's literary figures, including Margaret Wise Brown. He still get misty-eyed when he recalls their teamwork on books like *The Sailor Dog* (Golden) and her death at an early age. Other notable illustrating jobs have included works by Charlotte Zolotow, Margery Sharp, Randall Jarrell, George Selden, Mary Stolz, and, most recently, Jack Prelutsky.

When approached to re-illustrate Laura Ingalls Wilder's Little House books, Williams was at first dubious. He felt comfortable drawing talking animals, but was unsure about portraying realistic historical scenes. Besides, he says, "I had never been west of the Hudson River, and knew nothing of Laura Ingalls Wilder country."

At the insistence of Ursula Nordstrom, he studied the books. The first plan was for Williams to produce eight oil paintings for each book, sixty-four in all. In 1947, he set off on a trip to the American Midwest, to see if he could capture the aura he needed.

The first stop was at Rocky Ridge Farm near Mansfield, Missouri, where Laura and Almanzo Wilder still lived. He visited with them, experiencing awe that "here I stood with the hero and heroine of Mrs. Wilder's books." He found Laura Ingalls Wilder "very cheerful, sprightly, very much alive at eighty." He also found her informative and helpful but surprisingly unconcerned as to how he illustrated her books.

"I asked her if she would like to review my work and criticize it, but she never asked for changes," Williams remembers. He went on to visit all the sites of her books in Kansas, Minnesota, and South Dakota.

Despite the fact that the Wilder books contained "no spiders that talked," Garth Williams became absorbed in creating pictures for the eight-volume series. The original plan, to produce color paintings for the books, was cancelled due to costs, so Williams settled on the soft pencil-sketch style that he used for the hundreds of illustrations that grace the books. Much of his work was accomplished in Italy; by the time the Little House series was re-published in its new edition in 1953, six years had elapsed since he started the project.

During the 1950s, Garth Williams set up home and studio in Aspen, Colorado, when it was a quaint, quiet town with a single ski lift. With his second wife and four daughters, he immersed himself in family life and his work, which included writing as well as illustrating. His drawing and writing added prestige to the fledgling Golden Book series of high quality, low-cost children's titles pioneered by Simon & Schuster during the 1950s.

In 1958 Williams wrote and illustrated his much-admired but highly controversial book, *The Rabbits' Wedding* (Harper). The marriage of a black rabbit and a white rabbit was immediately seen by bigots as a fearfully subtle message during that early era of the civil-rights movement. Ironically, Williams denies any attempt at hidden meanings in the book. He says he simply tinted one rabbit black to distinguish it from the other. He still decries the mentality behind the unexpected hullabaloo his work elicited from book banners.

Of his illustrating craft, Garth Williams admits that his approach to a project is simple. "I won't do a book unless I like the manuscript," he insists. His initial reading of the material may suggest thirty or forty potential pictures. "To compose the pictures is very hard," he admits. "I look for all the action in the story; then I arrange forms and color. I always try to imagine what the author is seeing. Of course, I have to narrow down my ideas to the number of drawings I'm allowed, which might be as few as ten per book. I make a list of illustrations. When I see a picture, I write down the idea and a page number while I read the manuscript."

"Everyone thinks, 'How nice to illustrate children's books.' But I'm pragmatic. It's a job. My inspiration is my deadline. But when I start, the work usually goes quickly. I never get tired when I'm illustrating!"

Garth Williams's life and work shifted to Guanajuato, Mexico, during the 1960s and 1970s. There he bought, at a small cost, the four-hundred-year-old ruins of a Spanish silver mine. He rebuilt the picturesque structure, transforming it into a huge, fortresslike residence and studio. The compound includes a waterfall, fountains, cathedral arches, and a living room/dining room that seats 150 people. But for the artist-in-residence, the heart of the home is his mammoth studio, with its five work tables, nine skylights, piles of props, and accumulations of art work. His family sees the studio as impossibly messy and in need of organization, but Garth's benign silence on the matter indicates that a nonartist cannot possibly understand the proper ambiance of his working surroundings.

The long sojourns in Mexico gave some publishers and editors the notion that Garth Williams was retired or incommunicado, or both. He cites the series of garbled communications between himself and E. B. White that led to another artist illustrating White's *Trumpet of the Swan* (Harper) in 1970.

In 1974 Garth Williams married his present wife, Leticia; their courtship began during a portrait sitting. Although several decades separate them in age, the Mexican-born Mrs. Williams and her citizen-of-the-world husband make a successful team. "She's the best business manager I've ever had," Williams declares, obviously pleased to be relieved of some of the mundane requirements of life that interfere with his art. The Williams' only child, Dilys, is now in her early teens. The family currently divides its time between homes in Mexico and San Antonio, Texas.

Letty Williams keeps her husband's publishing deadlines straight, reminds him to be at the right place at the right time, and recently completed collecting and cataloguing the thousands of pieces of original artwork her husband has produced. "There is enough to fill the Metropolitan Museum of Art four times over," she says of the huge collection.

Garth Williams retains a zest that befits his roguish, sometimes irreverent, style. He's a master raconteur who can relate wild and improbable adventures with such diverse characters as Hitler and Picasso. He's a tireless charmer when he makes personal appearances around the country, glib but tender with his admirers. He's patient but incredulous when he autographs his way through mounds of books and always gracious when he accepts the adulation he receives.

When asked how he plans to spend his next ten years, Garth Williams says simply, "I'm going to have a lot of fun!" "And," he mentions humbly, "I hope I can be remembered for illustrating some of the best children's books of my time. Children need good books, and, I'm happy to say, they are getting better all the time. I hope I'm still illustrating them when I'm a hundred!"